SLA | GUIDELINES

CW01560814

Quality and Impact

Evaluating the Performance of your School Library

Elspeth Scott

Revised by:
Sally Duncan and Geoff Dubber

Series Editor: Geoff Dubber

Acknowledgements

The SLA would like to thank a number of people who have helped to create this new publication. Elspeth Scott for her original 2001 publication on self-evaluation, the text of which forms the basis of this new publication – thanks too for her helpful comments for this rewrite. We would also like to thank Sally Duncan and Geoff Dubber for the new material that they have contributed on this important topic, and of course Richard Leveridge and Jane Cooper for their excellent work for the Publications Team and with this particular new title.

Published by

School Library Association
1 Pine Court, Kembrey Park
Swindon SN2 8AD

Tel: 01793 530166 Fax: 01793 481182
E-mail: info@sla.org.uk
Web: www.sla.org.uk

Registered Charity No: 313660
Charity Registered in Scotland No: SC039453

Printed by Printondemand-Worldwide

Contents

66

'I'm always worried that measuring performance descends into bean counting and that the really important things can't be measured in that way.'

—*Elspeth Scott*

Data empowers people. People need information on how their schools are performing. They also need to understand how their school is performing against the best in class... It means robust self-evaluation and rigorous benchmarking. It means being honest about performance... it means learning from the best... without data [we] won't know.

—*Extracts from a speech by Leighton Andrews,*
Minister of Education Wales, February 2011

99

Why Measure Performance?

'The most effective librarians believe that the best way to influence head teachers is to ensure that the library is seen as pursuing the same improvement agenda as the rest of the school.... These librarians were happy to be held to account in relation to the school's targets for pupils' achievement and this led them into gathering evidence that showed the impact of the library on pupils' learning.'

—Philip Jarrett HMI. 'What can we learn from Good School Libraries?' *The School Librarian* vol.54, no.2, Summer 2006

Measuring performance is an important element of the work for everyone who runs a school library in either the primary or secondary phases of education. It provides an opportunity to reflect on what has happened over a period of time, looking at successes, trends and current developments. This activity will also provide an opportunity to identify areas which may need improvement. Above all, if tackled in a rigorous way, it can provide the evidence that you need to demonstrate how well the library and its staff are doing.

The more effectively you can prove the library's contribution to learning, the more the school is likely to value the library and what it has to offer. This increased value will also reflect on the role of the library staff. The act of giving your library a simple 'health check' or looking at specific aspects of your work is always useful too on a personal level. It may help to prove to others what you already know or feel:

- That the library is indispensable to the school and to learning

- That the library could usefully receive more funding to support learning across the school

- That more management support and even direct help can only help to improve library services.

The information and data that you gather will be important if you need to:

- explain your role and commitment to your senior leadership team, your line manager, teaching colleagues, associate staff, parents and the local community

- write a development plan and identify objectives and your next set of key tasks

- write an annual report

- put together budget proposals and justify them to senior management

- gather information, samples of work and general data for your library portfolio for OFSTED or any of the other national inspection/advisory services

- engage in any vital benchmarking activities and compare the services you offer with those of neighbouring schools so that your successes can be applauded and any difficulties clarified

and very importantly when you:

- demonstrate the role the library plays in raising pupils' attainment.

If clearly presented this information will provide unequivocal evidence of the quality and quantity of your work and will help to demonstrate the key role played by you and the library in supporting learning and teaching across the school. The data can be used to help your school colleagues to a greater understanding and appreciation of your work. It can also be used to 'prove the need' for more resources – perhaps more staffing, better accommodation or furnishings, increased ICT, improved book stock, or perhaps more space – many school libraries are too small. It can help you to identify changing patterns of use and customer needs. Most importantly, it can help to raise awareness of your role in the school and demonstrate how vital your role is in the learning that takes place.

For a number of years now English schools have had to examine their performance through the school's Self Evaluation Framework (SEF) and this has formed the basis of Ofsted inspections. Some schools featured the work of their school library in this important document, others didn't. Although the SEF will not be used for Ofsted inspections after September 2011 schools across the UK will still be expected to engage in self-evaluation in some form or another. School libraries will also be wise to continue to examine their own performance. After all, the school library is often one of the largest departments in the school. Even a small primary school library may well contains thousands of pounds worth of investment in terms of book stock and other resources; a secondary school library a good deal more. In the course of a week a school library usually deals with the learning and reading needs of a large number of pupils and staff, and often it is the department with least formal information about its performance.

Measuring in the right way can lead to a better service. If the governors, senior leadership team and the school at large don't understand your role and can't appreciate your contribution to teaching and learning, then the viability of the library, especially in the current economic climate, is put in doubt. So any improvement in the services offered, especially if they can be shown to impact on the learning and achievement of pupils will help to safeguard the library and the role of the library staff.

Performance measurement takes time. For school library staff already stretched by a multitude of daily and strategic tasks this may seem like an extra and even unwelcome burden. If it is to work for you it needs to be:

- focused in time and effort

- narrow in scope

- simple to operate

- it needs to support your current thinking and planning – either looking at your strengths or perhaps helping you to cope with some challenges.

At its most basic level measuring performance can be expressed as the process of answering a couple of simple questions:

1. How are we doing?

2. How do we know?

A third question can usefully be added to make sure that we do not rest on our laurels and let the library stagnate:

3. What are we going to do now?

Answering all three questions should help library staff and teaching staff to determine the library priorities and help towards turning good ideas – usually the library objectives – into good practice and key tasks for action.

The whole process needs to be discussed and agreed with your line manager as you will need their support if you are going to divert staff time from the usual duties. Depending on the information you need and the aspects that you wish to examine it may take a matter of weeks to gather and then review the evidence that you need. Don't rush at it or rush to complete it!

Tools and Toolkits

Performance can be measured in many ways but here are four useful sources of ideas to get you started – standards by which you can measure your own and the library's performance. It will be for you and your line manager to choose the standards which best suit your particular circumstances:

1. National standards. This information can be found in published library guidelines, such as those provided by the School Library Association[1] and from the members area of the SLA website at http://www.sla.org.uk/advice-and-support.php. For example see the advice about 'Book Stock Guidance'. The Chartered Institute of Library and Information Professionals (CILIP) also provide a whole range of advice about school libraries. *The CILIP Guidelines for Secondary School Libraries* is very helpful.[2] For example, the 'Recommended figures for library resourcing' in Chapter 5. Those who work in the primary sector will also find CILIP's *The Primary School Library Guidelines* useful.[3]

2. Local standards and measures developed by some school library services as part of their benchmarking activities. These will reflect local priorities and initiatives and maybe useful to supplement the national standards. Where they are available, these audits list key aspects of library provision and services. A wide sample of school libraries are then surveyed, the norm established for service levels and school libraries are invited to compare themselves against these benchmarks. It is worth remembering, however, that you are comparing your services against the average and not necessarily against an aspirational standard.

3. The aims and objectives set by the school itself and in particular those identified and agreed for the school library, which will have developed through consultation and through annual appraisal systems. In simple terms, this could just be comparing library performance data, both quantitative and qualitative year on year.

4. Standards and levels stated in published self-evaluation frameworks such as those listed in the next section.

It is important to remember that performance measurement is meant to encourage an objective rather than subjective view of the library and its success. To be meaningful it is vital to measure things that grow naturally from agreed objectives, so you need to know what you want to achieve before you start measuring in order to see whether you have met your

---

[1] See School Library Association. *SLA Standards for Secondary School Libraries*. 2011.

[2] CILIP, Barrett, Lynn, Douglas, Jonathan (eds). *The CILIP Guidelines for Secondary School Libraries*. CILIP, 2004. 978-1-85604-481-3.

[3] CILIP, rev. Douglas, J. *The Primary School Library Guidelines*. CILIP, 2002. 978-0-9543792-0-9. Available to download at: http://www.cilip.org.uk/get-involved/special-interest-groups/youth/publications/children/pages/primaryguidelines.aspx

targets. This means setting the library realistic and achievable goals which relate to its actual situation. It is also always useful to think about statements such as: 'we will have been successful when...'

> '....effective management is impossible without effective evaluation. It is the way in which the school librarian can learn what impact the library is having on the school, and how it contributes to the development of students...'
>
> —*The CILIP Guidelines for Secondary School Libraries*
> edited by Lynn Barrett and Jonathan Douglas, 2004.

Using published Self-Evaluation Frameworks

There are a number of well-established Self Evaluation Frameworks published which can help when you undertake your own self evaluation exercise. The most widely used are:

- *Improve Your Library: A Self Evaluation Process For Secondary School Libraries and Learning Resource Centres.* DFES, 2004.[4]

- *Improve Your Library: A Self Evaluation Process For Primary School Libraries.* DFES, 2004.[5]

- *Improving Libraries For Learners.* Scottish Library and Information Council, 2009.[6]

- *Inspiring Learning For All.* Museums Libraries and Archive Council, 2008.[7]

These may appear daunting at first glance because they are very comprehensive and cover a whole variety of the aspects of the work of a school librarian. Do remember that initially you are only expected to look at *one* chosen aspect of your service. They are also aspirational in that if you were to complete your self-evaluation investigation and find that you have achieved maximum scores in your chosen category or indeed in every category, you would be working in the 'ideal' library, although it may not be the best library for your school and your users.

---

[4] Hard copies of this may be available from your School Library Service. A useful copy of much of the material can be found at
http://www.informat.org/schoollibraries/downloads/ssecmplt.doc

[5] http://www.education.gov.uk/publications/standard/publicationdetail/page1/SLSEBP

[6] http://www.slainte.org.uk/files/pdf/slic/schoollibs/ImprovingLibsForLearners.pdf

[7] http://www.inspiringlearningforall.gov.uk/export/sites/inspiringlearning/resources/repository/Quick_checklist2.pdf

The two *Improve your Library* self-evaluation frameworks produced for England's schools come with related support materials, whether you work in the primary or secondary sectors, that recommend concentrating on just **one** strand at any given time. Take care to choose the strand which best fits in with your own priorities.

There is also some very useful school library self-evaluation material used in Northern Ireland. Produced as a pilot project in 2008 through school library authorities working in the regional Education and Library Boards, it is now used across the province. In the Belfast Education and Library Board area twenty one secondary school libraries have successfully completed their self-evaluation schedule and six more are currently employed. Currently the self-evaluation material has been transferred onto the LNI VLE.[8]

Birmingham City University also have a number of questionnaires on their website that may prove useful. These were originally produced by Anne-Marie Tarter, formerly school librarian at Ripon Grammar School. Library attitudes, Year 7 progress and use of the library by teaching staff all feature.[9]

Improving Libraries for Learners is a slim self-evaluation document designed for Scottish schools and is a follow up from their excellent and comprehensive *Libraries Supporting Learners*.[10] It links the school library self-evaluation into the Scottish Curriculum for Excellence. There is a good deal of useful information for all schools, however, and the 'signposts to effective practice' are particularly good as a checklist for identifying best practice:

> 2.1 Learners' experiences
>
> 5.3 Meeting learning needs
>
> 5.9 Improvement through self-evaluation

This model is set out as a grid with some useful headings that could be used in a school anywhere:

- How good are we now?

- How good can we be?

- What action will we take to improve current practice?

Inspiring Learning For All has some very useful downloads which can be adapted for your own circumstances. There are questionnaires, action plans and a useful 'Inspiring Learning' checklist. Some people find this easier to

---

[8] If you work in Northern Ireland and wish to use this material, then Sheelagh Rea at the School Library Service, Belfast Education and Library Board is a contact.

[9] http://www.ebase.bcu.ac.uk/projects/schoollibraries.htm (accessed 8 April 2011).

[10] Libraries Supporting Learners. Available at http://www.slainte.org.uk/files/pdf/slic/schoollibs/hgioslsl.pdf

use than the other frameworks. You will need to select the parts which are useful to you and fit in with the areas you want to evaluate as the documents cover museums, libraries and archives facilities and cater for all ages of customers.

Consider Your Focus

If you run a **secondary** school library you may like to consider focussing on the effectiveness of any of the following strands:

- reader promotion strategies and development programmes with specific classes or age ranges

- the library's induction programme for the new intake year

- the library's induction/transition programme used with 14+ exam classes

- the library's induction/transition programme used with 16+ students

- any induction programme used with new adults who work in school

- your general partnership working with teaching colleagues

- any partnership information literacy programmes with specific departments or with age groups

- out of hours study programmes

- work with the Sixth Form to promote and develop effective study habits, information literacy, etc.

- links to aid student transition/induction with local FE and HE institutions

- work with specific groups such as SEN, EAL and G&T students

- promotion of the local public library and local information networks

- The role of the library as the school's key information centre for teachers and students

- The library's role in supporting Continued Professional Development for teachers and learning support assistants

- The library environment – its layout and ambience

- the book stock – its currency and relevance to the school's curriculum

- any work to develop effective ICT searching skills

- The library's contribution to maintaining good behaviour throughout the school

- The library's role in developing responsible attitudes to the community, personal health or life style choices.

If you run a **primary** (infant or junior) school library then focussing on one of the following might be useful to you:

- strategies to support class teachers in promoting wider reading and reading for pleasure

- work in encouraging children to understand and use the local library network

- links with partner schools to develop transition and induction strategies

- work to develop key information literacy skills with different age groups; for example: alphabet and number skills, use of the Dewey Decimal Classification system, use of encyclopaedias, referencing skills, note making methods

- work to develop digital information literacy skills – use of search engines, key word searching and processing information

- work to promote safe and sensible internet use in line with the class teachers and school policies

- the library environment and ambience – furniture, fittings and facilities – is it good enough to support effective learning and reading enjoyment?

- the book stock – does it support the school's curriculum and is it relevant to the abilities and interest of the users?

- non-book materials – in what ways do they interest users and support learning needs?

- any work with SEN and EAL students – how do they benefit?

The Big Picture – obtaining an overview

Has anyone done any self-evaluation yet ? – I'm about to do ours and don't know where to start.

— A Bristol secondary school librarian, 2006

Our head likes statistics... I need to evaluate myself/facilities in order to drive forward the library in the future.

—A secondary school library, Birmingham, March 2009

My head is keen to develop our library. She has asked me to look carefully at the services we already offer and how we support learning, especially reading across the school, so we can move the library to the next stage. She wants some evidence for the Governors.

—A primary school library coordinator, 2009

The following model can help to get you started by looking at self-evaluation as a straightforward eight-step process.

Step 1: Recognise the need for and importance of carrying out some self-evaluation as a key part of the development process and perhaps skim read some of the relevant frameworks.

Step 2: Complete a school/library profile (see Appendix 1 for a secondary school and Appendix 2 if you work in a primary school).

Step 3: Choose an aspect of your service that you and your line manager/Head Teacher think most useful to reflect upon at this stage and consider using a colleague to help with this process. The partnership working should prove useful to both parties.

Step 4: Decide on the range and amount of evidence that you think you may need, consider ways that you (and perhaps your colleague) might collect this material and remember to pencil in a timescale for these activities.

Step 5: Collect your evidence – both data (quantitative) and information to show the quality of your current work and level of service.

Step 6: Using one of the descriptors or levels suggested by the published framework that you find most useful (see these in Appendix 4) – consider the level at which the library appears to be working and the reasons for your judgement.

Step 7: Using the information – decide on the ways in which you, with support from the school, might improve the aspect of work that you considered.

Step 8: Decide on your next possible self-evaluation activity and timescale.

Steps 1 to 3: Making a start

Step 1.

We are going to assume that you have already recognised the need for and the advantages of carrying out some self-evaluation and that you've had a read through some of the relevant framework material listed earlier. By this stage you will have a vision of what you want.

Step 2.

The next task is to complete the library profile sheet Appendices 1 or 2. This will give you a good idea of the range of your facilities and services – it will be a reference, a starting point from which to judge your library as a whole or to examine more closely the aspect that you wish to consider.

Step 3.
Choosing a focus for the evaluation.

- What general impression does the completed profile give you and your colleagues about the environment, provision and current use and profile of your library? Are there any particular areas that appear to need your attention?

- What action needs to be taken at this stage to improve/develop your library environment? Do have a look at other SLA Guidelines if you are unsure at this stage.[11]

- Select the area of the library service that you are going to evaluate. You can choose an area for improvement or an area which highlights the excellent work you are doing, depending on what you are aiming for with the self evaluation.

Go It Alone or work with a Colleague?

This may depend on your circumstances, personality, the scope of your investigation and the size and standing of your library. If it's done effectively self-evaluation can be a really useful activity, both to you as librarian (or perhaps as library coordinator in a primary school) and the school. It will take some work and some time and sharing the load, discussing ideas will usually be good for you and helpful to the colleague working with you who will learn a good deal about your library vision, ethos, range of services and general working standards. It is for you to pick your partner for this exciting work that may well say a good deal about you and the library that you have created and manage on a daily basis. Your team member may be your line manager, another colleague in school, a colleague or friend from a neighbouring school library or a member of your local Schools Library Service.

---

[11] See *Ideas and Designs* and *Visionary Spaces* in the Further Reading section of this publication

Step 4: Getting into the process

Step 4.
Decide on the range and quantity of material that you might need to make a judgement

Measuring the Measurable: How Are We Doing?

To begin the process of establishing the library's success you will need to gather evidence of what the library offers and what it is doing on a day-to-day basis in the area that you are considering.

This evidence will be in the form of 'performance measures' or 'performance indicators' that are either quantitative or qualitative.

> **A quantitative measure is a straightforward counting exercise to find a total; for example, the total number of pupils who use the LRC during a specific timescale.**

Quantitative measures are usually easy to gather, but they should not assume undue importance. They can be misleading because they give each piece of data or transaction equal importance.

> *There is a real danger that (school) librarians will count that which can be counted and ignore that which counts.*[12]

For example, one loan to a borrower and one information skills lesson both count as 'one'. The value, time taken, cost implications and 'value added' may be very different. Quantitative measures are sometimes described as 'hard measures'. They may include any of the following:

Accommodation and staffing

- the library's actual space

- a count of the furnishing and fittings – tables, chairs, ICT workstations, amount of shelving, display space, and so on

- hours in the week when the library is open for borrowing resources and for study

- hours when the library is staffed.

Finance

- total annual funding

- funding per pupil, perhaps by year group

---

[12] Quote from an article by Eileen Armstrong; *School Libraries in View* journal Spring 2004 Originally from Bob Usherwood *Rediscovering Public Library Management*. Facet Publishing, 1996.

- breakdown of expenditure for:

  - books/information resources

  - software/licences

  - hardware

  - other categories.

Services provided

- the scope and nature of lending facilities

- the range of ICT facilities and services offered

- your ability to answer reference enquiries

- your ability to work with ICT

- whether you carry out bibliographic and literature searches

- what links you have with outside agencies and the local community – for example, the local school library service, local library service, the careers service, inter-library loans

- whether you provide induction and INSET for teaching and support staff

- what links the library has with curriculum departments

- whether the library offers or obtain project loans

- the ability to offer advice on resource selection across the school

- the ability to maintain and develop the school's professional literature collection or resources for staff

- the nature of links with the school's careers library

- the facilities offered for study support/homework clubs

- the nature of work with pupil library volunteers and adult helpers.

Resources

Numbers of items:

- fiction books

- non-fiction books

- reference books

- non-book materials

- ICT software

- newspapers, magazines and journals

- online resources including ebooks.

Number of items:

- per pupil

- acquired during the last financial year

- edited and withdrawn.

Issue of items:

- total over a given period of time

- by category (for example, total fiction number)

- by age group/year group/gender group

- as percentage of stock

- as percentage on loan at one time.

Library use

During class time:

- by classes for induction

- by classes for research use/information skills – library staff working in partnership with teachers

- by groups

- for individual research or private study

- ICT use – web searching, e-mail use, other.

During free time:

- before school

- break times

- lunch times

- after school

- homework/study support.

For school and library focused activities such as book events, reading workshops, etc.

Use by the school adult community:

- number of visits by:
    - teachers
    - parents and volunteers
    - governors/school board members
    - learning support assistants
    - other adults.

Transactions (over an agreed time period)

- reference enquiries
- supported internet searches
- induction sessions for pupils and teaching staff
- information skills/research lessons in partnership with a teacher
- bibliographic/literature searches
- project loans borrowed from the local school library service
- project loans made up and loaned to curriculum departments
- inter-library loans organised
- the nature and range of the library's own planning meetings – line management meetings and others
- curriculum meetings attended by library staff
- pupils and staff accessing online resources.

Select the ones that will serve your purpose this time around. You may want to use quantative measures, for example, to show how many more visits the library gets now it has been refurbished or rearranged. This will not prove that the quality of the service has improved but if you combine the visit figures with how many books were borrowed and with comments from staff and students on the ease of finding what they want you can prove the quality of the improvements you have made and demonstrate them effectively to the school.

A qualitative measure is a measure which demonstrates the quality of the resources and services the library offers.

Although it is clearly easier to count and measure the tangible and visible – the quantitative – it is vitally important to go the extra step and include qualitative measures. These are essential for demonstrating the library's value to the school.

Qualitative performance measures are very much about 'value added': what impact does the library have on the quality of pupils' learning and attainment? This is the key issue and the other measures in a sense all focus on this one. As we all know, quality does not necessarily follow from quantity.

Qualitative measures include:

Resources

- relevance to pupils' ages, abilities and interests including suitability for pupils with special educational needs
- age
- condition
- sufficiency
- arrangement and accessibility
- layout and organisation
- clarity of signs and guiding
- nature and range of displays

Environment

Is it:

- welcoming, friendly and comfortable?
- conducive to active learning?
- suitable for multi-use – personal study, class use, private reading?

Staffing

- How good are your own professional training opportunities and what impact have they had on your work?
- How effective are your line management and appraisal procedures?
- How useful is the time spent working directly with pupils and staff?
- What is achieved in the time given to library administration?

Support for learning and teaching

- How good are the library induction sessions and information skills programmes – what do they achieve?

- To what extent is the library integrated into the whole-school learning policies and programmes?

- What is the library's contribution to

  - the school's national test results?

  - exam controlled assessment, coursework, project work and its marks?

  - encouraging and developing literacy and numeracy?

  - promoting and encouraging wider reading for pleasure and interest?

  - developing ICT skills?

  - developing lifelong learning skills?

  - school activities – such as book events and activities weeks

  - school ethos?

If you have chosen, for example, to look at the library's contribution to raising achievement in History you could concentrate on how good the resources are that you provide for History, how you let pupils and staff know how to access them, how you work with the History department to teach the skills pupils need to research and present work effectively and how this feeds into improving attainment in internal and external assessments of those pupils.

Step 5: Collect your evidence – how do we know?

Evidence falls into three categories:

1. Information which already exists

This may be in the form of 'hard measures': information about the school – number on roll, number of pupils in different classes or year groups, and so on. It will also include data that you use as everyday working information, perhaps issue statistics, use by classes on a regular basis, the amount of time you are available in the library on a weekly basis, and the amount of time you have for dealing with library administration. It should also include information that you have collected in your current library policy file and ongoing 'evidence box' or library portfolio.

2. Data which can be easily discovered from existing information

This might include the balance of use by different subject departments by examining the library booking information; the number of fiction volumes used by a specific year group; or the number of pupils using your after-school study support facilities. This information can often be easily obtained by using the 'reports' function on your library management system. If you work in a smaller primary school without one then some counting from paper based records will be useful.

3. Data which needs to be collected specifically

It is important to realise that gathering evidence does not have to be a huge extra burden. Often minor amendments to existing practice will enable useful information to be recorded. It is essential to record only the information you will need. This of course means referring back to the library's policy, development plan and key objectives. If you have an automated issue and catalogue system it is worth looking to see what extra information this may be able to provide. However, some extra planning may be required here.

Collecting specific data

The first and perhaps most obvious qualitative measure that might be needed for this process concerns the resources. Although you may have counted the actual number of different categories, it is the quality of the materials that matters.

If resources are your focus then they should be measured by age, condition and relevance to the school's curriculum. Age and condition of resource surveys are relatively easy to organise. See the SLA Guidelines *Shelf Life, Shelf Matters* or *Making a Start With Your Primary School Library* for ways to go about this activity. For 'relevance to the school's curriculum' you will need a detailed breakdown of which topics are taught in which year – a curriculum grid – and match your stock to those topics, bearing in mind that you will need to meet a range of reading levels and experiences for each set of pupils.

The second qualitative measure to consider is how the library is used. There are various ways of recording library use.

1. Keeping a diary or log book

Many school libraries already keep a **diary** for recording bookings for class use and other appointments. This can also be used to record:

- 'five bar gate' counts of enquiries

- any comments made in passing by pupils and staff about the resources – such as a teacher commenting on the fact that 'the class worked well today'; a pupil's comment about the usefulness of a resource; someone's failure to find the information they needed; or any problems encountered with a piece of equipment. Record the challenging as well as the positive; and it is worth expanding cryptic notes if you can find the time. Instead of simply 'three groups from Mr Smith's class', you could usefully include 'class working on their "Animals" project', or 'class researching Viking boat building'. For a secondary school, the entry might perhaps be 'Sixth Form group researching their extended essay', or 'group planning a presentation about the local area'. This doesn't take much longer to write, but the extra detail records valuable information and evidence of library use.

- head counts of out-of-class use at identified breaks and lunch-times or over a specific time span.

A useful extension to the diary is a **log book** in which pupils and staff record their use of library facilities. One secondary school librarian asks everyone who uses the library over an agreed period of time, to complete an entry in 'the silver book'. This records date, time, name, class and purpose of the visit. It can also be completed when they leave to record the success or any problems with the visit. It can incorporate details of resources and facilities used (see Appendix 3). A research slip can be used to record similar sorts of information if that makes more sense in your particular situation.

There are, of course, practical issues with any recording system. A log jam of busy, noisy pupils waiting to complete information of this sort is not practical. Choose a specific time to do it when you are sure that numbers will be manageable or when you have the support of other members of staff to help.

In a busy primary or secondary school library it is not reasonable or desirable for absolutely everything to be recorded.

It will pay to give careful consideration to the timing of data collection. The imminence of exams, or events of different sorts, can give you atypical results. It may be better to choose a particular performance measure – one where you need to prove a point, or perhaps one you haven't recorded before. Focus on it for a longer time span (perhaps a fortnight or a month) and record all transactions and comments relating to this.

2. Keeping an evidence box or library portfolio

It is extremely helpful to keep evidence that might be useful for evaluation or simply to demonstrate the range and curriculum input of the library.

Do think about collecting a selection of the following:

- timetables and booking sheets
- copies or photocopies of completed research slips and project planners
- worksheets/assignment sheets from pupils and departments
- examples of annotated pupil work resulting from library use or use of library resources, perhaps as photocopies if the pupil or teacher still requires the actual work
- photographs and videos of library use, displays, events
- feedback forms and completed questionnaires from staff and pupils about use for a specific topic or project
- notes of any comments made by pupils or staff about the library and their use of it
- observations and comments made by individuals or groups of pupils
- details of involvement with local, national or school based book awards
- copies of library newsletters or contributions to school communications in one form or another.

This information will help to provide you with data, both quantitative and qualitative.

Collecting evidence for the impact on learning

The impact on learning is arguably the most important performance measure of all. Unfortunately it is often the most difficult one to measure, and the most elusive, for a number of reasons:

- The library contributes to and supports the work of teaching staff, but usually does not have a separate element in the final work

- The results of work done in the library or using library resources will be integrated into the pupil's final presentation and may be difficult to isolate

- A successful induction session, information skills programme, or curriculum research activity will, hopefully, result in the internalisation of these skills and evidence may be difficult to quantify

- There is little tradition or methodology for evaluating and measuring the library's impact upon learning in most schools.

Measuring these rather less tangible aspects of success is, however, vitally important. If the school has a whole-school information/learning skills policy, or if library staff are involved in delivering induction sessions, working alongside teachers in curriculum partnership work or in delivering the traditional library/information skills programme, then it is important to consider:

- whether there is evidence for the development of skills

- how motivated the pupils are when engaging with the work

- the quality of the completed work and how the library contributed to that quality.

In order to do this you will need to identify and formulate key objectives or 'performance targets' against each criteria you wish to measure.

For example, to measure the motivation of the pupils, you may need to set yourself a series of statements, such as: 'Pupils are keen, interested and on task for at least 50 per cent of the time.' Statements of this sort need to be discussed with teaching staff before being used. You can use them to measure the pupils you observe against the statement and you may find that 60 per cent, perhaps more, of the class fall into this category.

To show evidence for the support of skills development – perhaps Locating and Gathering Skills – could be: 'Y9/S3: all pupils should know how to use the library catalogue and the Dewey system to locate library resources on open access.' You may find that only 50 per cent of those observed could carry out this task. But this evidence will be useful in setting goals in your

Development Plan, as you can form strategies for improving this figure to 75 per cent, for example.

Some indication of the impact on learning can be gained by looking at patterns of use. If a department or perhaps class teacher continues to use the library to support a unit of work or general curriculum topic, then it is a fair deduction that they consider its use valuable and the resources relevant and useful. You can easily check this assumption by asking the relevant member of staff – do not forget to write down what they say! This can be a practical starting point for examining the ways in which the library and the library staff are supporting the unit of work and measuring the benefits the pupils gain from the experience.

Important too in measuring quality is for library staff to have opportunities to become involved at the beginning and the end of a piece of work. They will then understand the planning and have a clearer picture of the learning objectives, of what the pupils achieved, and how this information was recorded.

Simple observation can be a useful, if time-consuming, tool. Again it is essential to have clear performance targets and criteria before you start and careful design of a record sheet will be most helpful here. You could measure:

- the amount of time a pupil or a group spend on task

- locating and gathering skills; pupils looking for special resources or topic information

- use of ICT equipment.

Using your digital camera or camcorder can help to capture the enthusiasm, mood and interest level of your library users, so long as the pupils under review don't play to the camera!

What do your customers think about the services you offer?

Asking people for their opinions can be off-putting and there is always a tendency for them to be kind and polite and tell you what they think you want to hear. It is always worth reminding them that constructive feedback is useful to you as it can lead to improved library services which are more effective in serving their needs.

There are a number of ways opinions can be gathered:

Surveys can take a broad look at the library services and success, but are usually more effective if focussed on an area of particular concern, to you or to others. It is probably sensible to start with a small section of the school population at first as any attempt to survey the entire school, even a medium-sized primary school needs support from the senior management team to emphasise the importance of the activity. Many secondary school library staff make use of SurveyMonkey (http://www.surveymonkey.com/), an online survey tool, to gather this type of information.

Questions need to be carefully designed and specifically targeted and it is useful to conduct a small-scale trial before using them in a full-scale survey. It is generally better to have several shorter questionnaires or surveys over a period of time than one enormous one that is daunting to both teachers and pupils. Make the meaning of your questions absolutely clear and keep them to two sides of A4 paper at the very maximum. If you are asking colleagues or pupils to grade performance, perhaps on a scale of 1 to 5, make sure your target audience understands the scaling system you are offering and is using the same criteria. You do not want to get all 5s (poor) when people meant to judge your service as 1 (excellent) but they did not read or understand the instructions.

To persuade colleagues to complete an evaluation form on a recent INSET course, each form was numbered, completed forms were raffled at the end of the session, and prizes were awarded. Participation was 100 per cent!

Be sure to thank participants, and remember that feedback from the information you have gathered needs to be disseminated quickly if you want to maintain goodwill and interest – ideally in the form of actions that will benefit users.

'Snapshot surveys' can be a quick way of getting an overview of user perceptions. How about a brief sheet asking pupils and staff to list the five best things about their school library? You could also ask them to list the five worst things about it, and the actions you need to take to encourage them to make better or more frequent use of the library. This isn't daunting for users and can produce very revealing information. In a secondary school where all staff and one register class (tutor group) in each year group (targeted through social education/PHSE) were asked to complete a sheet of this type, there was surprising unanimity about the results and lots of positive comments.

Feedback forms can be used in various contexts, perhaps at the end of a unit of work which the class has been doing in the library. Forms of this type should address issues relating to pupils' learning and attainment as well as the quality of the resources. They can be used to better inform you about the quality or use of individual resources or equipment, booking arrangements, Internet websites. Ask pupils as well as staff to complete feedback forms. Their comments and suggestions can be illuminating and they are often devastatingly honest!

Interviews and discussions can be formal, perhaps during a piece of curriculum work done in partnership with a teacher, or informal and casual; but it is important to take notes at any meeting of this nature. Don't rely on your memory! Minutes of departmental/year group meetings may also provide useful information and opinion about the library and its use.

Step 6: Making a judgement

Having gathered your range of quantitative and qualitative evidence you now need to decide if you have enough to make an informed judgement about the area of your service that you were focused on.

At this stage and as you make a judgement do seek support – taking these decisions by yourself may be difficult – working alone you may well judge yourself and your services rather too critically, or perhaps give too much weight to factors beyond your control. Try to be as objective as possible. This evaluation is after all a pointer to the future.

Step 7: Using the information – what are we going to do now?

'Self-evaluation is not an end in itself, any more than an inspection is. It should be a guide to the way forward and can be used to bring about practical improvements and, possibly, better funding.'

— *Sheila Percival. 'I know where I'm going: a pilot project looks at self-evaluation for school libraries' The School Librarian, volume 53, number 2, summer 2005.*

'Five WELB schools... have recently completed an Inter-Board school library self-evaluation pilot... we can report that all schools derived great benefit from their participation. School library staff found their self confidence increasing and the role of the library was highlighted in a new way'

—*School Library Service newsletter, Autumn 2008. Western Education and Library Board Northern Ireland*

Now the information has been gathered it is important that it works effectively for you. Use the evidence to support the case you're making for the library and the library staff. You can use it to create **performance indicators** which are a powerful way of demonstrating success.

'Performance measures' measure what is actual – perhaps the total fiction stock level, or the number of issues in a month, or the number of uses of a specific CD or DVD in a week. They tend to be numerical and usually do not include any library impact on learning and teaching, quality of work, or put the library's workload into a meaningful context. Skilfully combining two or more performance measures to make a 'performance indicator' can create a much more powerful message.

A performance indicator is a combination of two or more measures that demonstrate the performance or success of a specific aspect of your service.

For example, take the total number of fiction books on your shelves, match it with the number of fiction books on loan, and you have a more powerful figure which shows the percentage of stock on loan at a given time. Another example would be to highlight the number of borrowers in a particular year group and match against the total pupil population of that group to show how much use that group makes of the library. Again you will arrive at a very useful percentage figure. One more might be the time in which the library ICT is in use matched against its total availability. This may well provide useful data to reinforce your requests for another workstation or two!

If you've taken part in a local school library service benchmarking activity and compared your services and performance with those of other schools, now is the time to shout about it – to demonstrate your high placing, or perhaps to demonstrate your lowly position in the table. Perhaps your average funding per pupil per year is the lowest in the area, or your stock is in the worst condition. Now is the moment to tell your head about your place in the league table and to state the information clearly in library documentation for wider dissemination!

Performance indicators can be used to good effect to support your case in many library documents, especially:

- an annual report

- a library development plan

- budget proposals

- OFSTED/inspection briefing papers

- information for the school's prospectus.

The library's **annual report** is a statement of 'where we are now' and 'what we've been doing recently'. The library in both a primary or secondary school is a major investment and everyone who has responsibility for one should seize every opportunity to justify the money spent on it by demonstrating its general success, its impact on the life of the school, and its contribution to learning.

The information gathered is of crucial importance in showing the library's success and current standing, and also its areas of need. Detailed statistical information can usefully be included as an appendix to the main report, but remember that many people will skip over the extras unless they are clearly and attractively presented. Try to keep the report concise and clearly written and aim for no more than two or three sides of A4 paper for the main body of the report. If you are asked to provide an annual report for a primary school library it will probably be even more succinct, but it is nevertheless a very worthwhile activity and very much a public relations as well as an effective future planning tool.

It is essential to support your statements, comments and opinions on the year's happenings, with evidence from the data gathered as you outline the library's achievements and draw attention to problem areas and challenges yet to be addressed. The report should clearly mark progress, substantial or otherwise, made against the vision and objectives set out in the library development plan.

The annual report will also give you the opportunity to highlight achievements and events.

In any library's annual report it is useful to include some of the following:

- recent achievements, purchases and current trends/pressures

- comments arising from any recent inspection or advisory visits

- interesting new book stock

- new ICT software and hardware, its use and reasons for its purchase

- new courses offered

- pressures of use matched against staffing

  - number of issues (don't forget to include project loans)

  - number of users matched against the total school population

  - budget figures matched against pupil numbers

  - benchmarking information

- the work of the Library Committee

- attendance at school meetings – curriculum (especially literacy groups), parents, governors, INSET

- club activity with a library focus – reading, study support, and so on

- work with pupil and adult library volunteers – remembering to mention them by name

- staff and pupil induction programmes

- new developments

- reorganisation of resources and the reasons behind it

- response to educational initiatives

- resource evaluation related to government and school curriculum changes

- partnership work with teachers and changes to information skills programmes

- new links with outside organisations.

Remember to include any special events:

- author visits

- reader development work, shadowing Carnegie or Greenaway activities, for example, or participating in local book award schemes

- book fairs and book events

- special displays, especially if linked to curriculum work

- competitions and quizzes

- sponsorship links.

The professional development of the library staff could be mentioned:

- courses attended at your local SLS, at the SLA, and elsewhere

- qualifications gained

- contribution to school or wider INSET

- contribution to local and national professional organisations.

Discuss your draft annual report with your line manager before it is widely circulated. It should be a good promotional tool, and copies could usefully be distributed to:

- the head

- the senior management team

- teaching colleagues

- adult and older volunteer pupil helpers

- your local school library service

- named copies to the governors/school board, with an offer to attend one of their meetings to discuss it

- if suitable, a copy could be posted on the school's website or VLE as information to parents/carers.

Above all, remember that the annual report is your opportunity to celebrate your successes and to highlight the steps you plan to take next.

Performance indicators that might go into your annual report include:

1. To show how the library fulfils its role in the school:

   - % of staff and pupils who use the library

   - % of staff and pupils who use the library over a week

   - % of staff and pupils who consider the library as essential to their work

   - % of staff who think that the library is essential to supporting literacy.

2. To highlight areas of concern, use:

   - % of requests not adequately satisfied

   - issue statistics and trends for different year groups, classes, fiction/non-fiction divide

- resource target (per pupil) against actual figures

- use of ICT equipment compared to the demand use of library ICT for uses that are essentially non-library

- % of users unable to find seats for study during the lunch times of a typical week in November or February.

3. To report on achievements and the library's value to the school:

- % of pupils in specific year groups achieving competence at certain skills

- % of pupils who were involved in a specific project/event and the satisfaction rate

- extracts of work done by pupils using library resources

- sample anecdotes and comments from questionnaires and evaluation forms, personal statements from staff and pupils.

The **library development plan** (LDP or LIP – the terms Development Plan and Improvement Plan are interchangeable) arises naturally from matching four sets of documents:

- the school's development/improvement plan

- the library's aims and objectives (library policy document)

- the performance measures that you have been using and any benchmarking activities or comparisons you have been making with published standards

- inspection criteria and information.

For further advice, see the SLA guidelines listed under Further Reading:

- *Paperwork Made Easy: Policy Making and Development Planning for the Secondary School Library.* (Samples of this paperwork are available at http://www.sla.org.uk/paperwork.php)

- *Practical Paperwork: Policy Making and Development Planning for the Primary School Library.*

Start by identifying the library's strengths and don't be modest about these. Remember to include your performance measurement activities. These in themselves show library staff to be reflective, analytical and concerned with service delivery. Next look for areas which are satisfactory and need only maintenance. Finally consider areas where improvement is needed. Some librarians like to carry out this thinking by doing a SWOT analysis – listing the Strengths, Weaknesses, Opportunities and Threats to the library – and discussing it with their line manager.

Once the areas which need improvement have been identified, prioritise them. Organise them into three groups: those that need immediate attention, those for the longer term, and those perhaps beyond your immediate control but where you need to exert pressure and influence – to change the library's carpet perhaps, or improve the heating system.

Identify projects, or steps to tackle the issues. Set targets with time limits – short, medium or longer term – for each:

- 'review science stock in light of changes to the GCSE exams'

- 'consider work with Extended Project Qualifications students to provide effective information/models for referencing/plagiarism'

- 'develop some library pages on the school's Intranet using Year 5 library children' or

- 'check and evaluate some Key Stage 1 websites for use with the Y2s'.

Major initiatives will usually be longer term, but in any major project it is morale boosting to build in a number of TATTs (Tiny Achievable Tickable Targets). It might be helpful to produce a separate action plan for a project/initiative of this size, dividing the project into manageable steps and detailing the resources, people and time-scale involved. Setting dates helps to keep you focused and turns good intentions into good practice. It also builds in times for monitoring and a review of progress.

It is useful if the LDP is drawn up in a similar style to the school's development plan (this may already be school policy). Remember though that it is a working document, not just one for your library file. It should be distributed to senior management and perhaps heads of department. If you have advertised what you are trying to do, there is a greater incentive to achieve it.

It can be helpful to put a large copy of your term's targets on to flip chart paper. Display this in your library office, or somewhere where it will remind you and your helpers of the tasks in hand, and tick off whatever has been accomplished.

As you monitor and evaluate the LDP you will quickly identify areas which need to be looked at in the next phase of development planning.

Performance indicators that you might consider putting into your LDP include:

- % of library users in the school, compared with non-users – pupils, staff and departments

- % of users from different age ranges

- % of pupils who use or who are interested in using study support facilities

- % of users who are satisfied/not satisfied with your range and quality of resources

- % of pupils who use the library at lunch-time

- number of days/sessions when you have an overcrowding problem

- staff time spent for admin compared with staff time for pupils/enquiries

- levels of satisfaction with resources and services among staff using the library with classes

- areas of the curriculum served/not served adequately by the library

- % of time found for professional development and liaison with curriculum staff

- % of time spent in a typical week upon, or number of queries concerned with, ICT equipment repair and maintenance issues

- number of pupils queuing to use the library in a typical winter weekday lunch-time

- % of overdue books not returned within four weeks

- % of a sample of fiction stock unused over a period of one year.

Budget proposals constitute another key annual document that all library staff need to create and use as a working document. As with the LDP, budget discussion, creation and monitoring is cyclical and can usefully include performance measures and indicators to illustrate and explain the reasons behind the budget proposals.

Performance indicators you might consider putting into your budget planning include:

- amount of money allocated per pupil per year for resources, perhaps split between fiction, non-fiction and ICT

- % of funding for different types of resource – books, online resources, ICT software, ICT consumables, newspapers, professional training

- budget comparisons with schools of similar sizes and your position in any benchmarking activities

- quantity and quality of resources measured against local and national standards and guidelines – perhaps highlighting your lack of quality fiction for a specific age or ability range

- the possible number of resources you can borrow from your local school library service over a year, compared with the number of resources you could buy for your library with the same amount of money.

Inspection papers. Currently Inspecting teams will only visit the library if it is an integral part of the focus of the inspection. Things they will be looking for if they do inspect it will be:

In the primary school library

- the way it promotes higher levels of literacy

- the way it provides for personal study

- its contribution to encouraging pupils to read widely and confidently

- the extent to which pupils value reading as a source of pleasure and information

In the secondary school library

- the way it promotes higher levels of literacy

- its support for effective and challenging teaching

- the way it provides a multi-media resource for personal study

- its contribution in enabling and encouraging pupils to read widely and confidently

- the extent to which pupils value reading as a source of pleasure and information.

The team forming these judgements can be supported by information about the range of performance measures that you have used. These can include:

- measures of library provision:
  - staff hours

- opening hours

- resource levels

- budget figures

- measures of library use:

    - % of users across the school – staff/departments/pupils

    - issue statistics and recent trends

    - use of ICT equipment

    - number of pupils using the library at specific free and curriculum times

- measures of library effectiveness:

    - % of satisfied users – staff and pupils

    - % of regular fiction borrowers

    - details of curriculum work done with departments

    - samples of pupil work

    - details of reading promotions

    - anecdotes from pupils about reading promotions

    - details of reading events

    - details of work with special needs/learning support staff and pupils

    - responses from a questionnaire following staff or pupil induction programmes.

Step 8 – what next?

Congratulations! A task well achieved. Hopefully your school will have a more effective service and your school's management team will be able to understand and more clearly appreciate the work that you do. Take a break to reflect on the whole process and then once you've considered your school and library priorities for the coming months, choose another area to evaluate.

Conclusion

Measuring the library's success, whether for a primary or secondary school, is undoubtedly a most useful activity. It should be focused on providing evidence to support your thinking and the library's contribution as a major player in school learning and teaching.

Initially seen as demanding, and perhaps even a little threatening and time consuming, measuring success can be enlightening and invigorating and a catalyst for change and development. It can give you some of the facts and figures that you need to prove your effectiveness while, at the same time, giving you the evidence to push home your concerns. This evidence can impress senior managers and decision-makers and give your discussions and library documentation increased authority and importance.

And finally:

Don't be frightened by it

Don't try to measure everything at once

Don't let it assume undue importance

Don't try to do it all by yourself

Do start from where you are

Do involve other people

Do be honest with yourself and other people

Do share good practice

Do try itl

Appendix 1

Profile of the School and its Secondary School Library

Name of School

Part A – Profile of the School

Type of school

Additional information – status, specialisms etc.

Profile of students

Age range of students	
Number of Roll Lower School Upper School	
By Gender	Male: Female:
Students with EAL Students with SEN	
Students eligible for free school meals	

Student academic performance

No of students at Level 4 and above on entry to school		
No of students at Level 3 and below on entry to school		
Students achieving 5 good GCSEs or equivalent	No	%
No of students leaving education at 16		
Students achieving 3 good GCE A Levels or equivalent	No	%
6th formers going into Higher Education	No	%

Part B – Profile of the Library

Library Staffing

Job title and role	Qualifications/training	Hours employed per week – Term time	Hours employed per week – School holidays

Links between library staff and teaching staff – shared meetings, training etc.	INSET provided by library staff to school colleagues

Access

Number of hours opening to users per week – class time	
Number of hours open to users – non-teaching time	
Number of non ICT seats available	
Number of ICT workstations/laptop spaces available	
Number of library staff on duty at any time	
Ratio of staff to students – class time	
Ratio of staff to students – non-teaching time	

Funding

Library total budget in this current financial year	£
Compare the above figure to the previous year's budget	
Total budget per student during this current year	£
Funding allocated by the school	£
Funding gained from other sources	£
% of budget spent on: 　Books 　Fiction... 　Non-fiction... 　Reference... 　Newspapers, magazines etc...................... 　Online resources...................................... 　ICT hardware... 　ICT software and support......................... 　ICT consumables..................................... 　School Library Service sub........................ 　Subscriptions.. 　Other...	

Resources

Total number of books.....................

% over 10 years old........................

Number of computers......................

Number with internet access...............

Range of other digital resources

LRC resources held elsewhere in the school

Link with Careers Dept resources

Use

% of teaching staff who actively use the library and its resources

% of time the LRC is booked for lessons that make use of library resources

% of time the LRC ICT workstations are used for subject use

Average number of users per day

Average number of Sixth Form Private

Study students per day

Average number of after school users as part of a formal or informal homework club

How many students currently have an item on loan?

Total number of items loaned over the previous 12 months

What % of the students could be classed as non-users?

Support offered to exam classes

Library after school activities

Library activities for this last 12 months – book events etc

Outline the information skills or reader development programmes offered to one year group over the last 12 months

Promotion and Displays

Does the LRC feature in the school's prospectus and various other curriculum information handouts?	
Does the LRC feature on the school's website and VLE?	
Do library staff attend Open Evenings and school parents' information and curriculum meetings?	
How many different curriculum based displays have been organised in the LRC in the last 12 months?	

Support

Line management structure/appraisal system etc.
Support from School Library Service
Support obtained from the School Library Association
Support from other information services – public library etc.
Links with partner primary school library staff and part of cross-sector library induction strategies
Links with neighbouring school library staff
Links with neighbouring FE, HE and university libraries for reference and induction programmes
Other

(adapted from DfES Secondary School Library Self-Evaluation materials)

Appendix 2

Profile of the School and its Primary School Library

Name of School

Part A – Profile of the School

Type of school (church, independent etc.)

Additional information

Profile of children

Age range of students		
Number of Roll Infant Dept. Junior Dept.		
By Gender	Boys	Girls
children with EAL children with SEN		
children eligible for free school meals:		

SATS

No of children obtaining different SAT levels at KS 2	Level 1 and below Level 2 Level 3	
No of children obtaining different SAT levels at KS4	Level 2 and below Level 3 Level 4 Level 5	

Part B – Profile of the Library

Library Staffing

Job title and role	Qualifications/training	Hours employed per week – Term time	Hours employed per week – School holidays

Line management structure for library staff	Links between library staff and teaching staff shared meetings, training etc.

Access

Number of hours opening to users per week – class time	
Number of hours open to users – non-teaching time	
Number of non ICT seats available	
Number of ICT workstations/laptop spaces available	

Funding

Library budget in this current financial year	£
Compare the above figure to the previous year's budget	
Total budget per child during this current year	£
Funding allocated by the school	£
Funding gained from other sources	£

% of budget spent on: Books Fiction…………………………………………… Non-fiction……….………………………….. Reference…………………………………...... Newspapers, magazines etc…….…………..… Online resources……………………….……… ICT hardware…………………………………… ICT software and support…………………..….. ICT consumables…………………………...….. School Library Service sub……………..……… Subscriptions……………………...………….. Other………………………………………….	

Resources	
Total amount of book stock per child (including stock held from School Library Service)	
Total number of books..................... % over 10 years old.........................	
Number of computers..................... Number with internet access…...........	
Range of other digital resources available for use in the library	
Library resources held elsewhere in the school	

Use	
% of class teachers who actively use the library and its resources to support curriculum learning and teaching	
% of time that the library is booked for lessons that make use of library resources	
% of time the library ICT workstations are used for library purposes	
Average number of voluntary users per day ie. not those doing class book swaps as part of a lesson	
Average number of after school users as part of a formal or informal homework/library or reading club	
What % children regularly borrow books and/or other library resources?	
Total number of items loaned over the previous 12 months	

Library after school activities

Library activities for this last 12 months – book events etc.

Outline the information skills or reader development programmes offered to one year group over the last 12 months

Promotion and Displays

Does the library feature in the school's prospectus and various other curriculum information handouts?
Does the library feature on the school's website and VLE?
How many different curriculum based displays have been organised in the LRC in the last 12 months?

Support

Support provided from School Library Service
Support provided from the School Library Association
Support provided from other information services – public library etc.
Links with partner secondary school library staff and part of cross-sector library induction strategies
Links with neighbouring primary school library staff
Other

(adapted from DfES School Library Self-Evaluation materials)

Appendix 3

Log book structure

Date	Lesson	Staff	Class	Subject	Activity	Comment

Appendix 4

Descriptors/levels used in a variety of published frameworks

Scotland's *Improving Libraries for Learners* [a]

- How Good Are We Now – what evidence do we have for our strengths and areas for development?

- How Good Can We Be?

- What action will we take to improve current practice?

Scotland's *Libraries Supporting Learners* [b]

- Level 6 – Excellent. Very best practice and experiences.

- Level 5 – Very Good. Major strengths. Very few weaknesses, if there are any do not diminish pupils' experiences.

- Level 4 – Good. Important strengths that have a significant impact. Areas for improvement diminish the quality of pupils' experience in some way.

- Level 3 – Adequate. Strengths just outweigh weaknesses. Pupils have access to basic level of provision.

- Level 2 – Weak. Weaknesses that are important enough to have a negative impact on the quality of pupils' experiences.

- Level 1 – Unsatisfactory. Major weaknesses in provision. Pupils' experience is at risk in significant respects.

England's level descriptors used in the DES *Improve Your Library: A Self Evaluation Process for Secondary School Libraries and Learning Resource Centres*[c]

- Excellent

- Good

- Intermediate

- Emergent

- Needs development

England's level descriptors used in the DES *Improve Your Library: A Self Evaluation Process for Primary School Libraries*[d]

- Excellent or very good: the library is strong in this area.

- Good: the library addresses this area well, but some improvement is possible.

- Satisfactory: The library is doing work in this area, but further improvement is needed.

- Needs development: little or no action has been taken in this area and provision lacks impact; urgent intervention is required.

Northern Ireland's *Self-Evaluation of the School Library Pilot Toolkit*[e]

- Grade 1   Almost/nearly all there   75% or more

- Grade 2   Most   65 – 74%

- Grade 3   A majority of   55 - 64%

- Grade 4   A significant minority   45 - 54%

- Grade 5   A minority   40 - 44%

- Grade 6   Very small/a small number of   Less than 40%

[a]   *Improving Libraries for Learners*. Scottish Library and Information Council, 2009, pp13–14.

[b]   *Libraries Supporting Learners*. Scottish Library and Information Council, 2005, p8. Available at http://www.slainte.org.uk/files/pdf/slic/schoollibs/hgioslsl.pdf.

[c]   *Improve Your Library: A Self Evaluation Process for Secondary School Libraries and Learning Resource Centres*. DFES, 2004, p3.

[d]   *Improve Your Library: A Self Evaluation Process for Primary School Libraries*. DFES, 2004, p6.

[e]   *Self-Evaluation of the School Library Pilot Toolkit*. 2007-2008, pp34-36.

Further reading

Accounts Commission for Scotland. *Measuring Up to the Best: A Manager's Guide to Benchmarking.* 1999. Available at: http://www.audit-scotland.gov.uk/docs/local/pre1999/nr_9901_managers_guide_benchmarking.pdf

CILIP, Barrett, Lynn, Douglas, Jonathan (eds). *The CILIP Guidelines for Secondary School Libraries.* CILIP, 2004. 978-1-85604-481-3.

CILIP, rev. Douglas, J. *The Primary School Library Guidelines.* CILIP, 2002. 978-0-9543792-0-9. Available at: http://www.cilip.org.uk/get-involved/special-interest-groups/youth/publications/children/pages/primaryguidelines.aspx

Convention of Scottish Local Authorities (CoSLA): Education and Cultural Services Forum. *Standards for School Library Services in Scotland: A Framework for Developing Services.* 1999.

Dewe, Michael. *Ideas and Designs: Creating the Environment for the Primary School Library.* School Library Association, 2007. 978-1-903446-39-3.

Dubber, Geoff and Lemaire, Kathy. *Visionary Spaces: Designing and Planning a Secondary School Library.* School Library Association, 2007. 978-1-903446-38-6.

Duncan, Sally. *Making a Start with your Primary School Library.* School Library Association, 2010. 978-1-903446-55-3.

Harrison, Kay and Admas, Tricia. *Practical Paperwork: Policy Making and Development Planning for the Primary School Library.* School Library Association, 2007. 978-1-903446-37-9.

Jarrett, Philip, HMI. 'What can we learn from Good School Libraries?' *The School Librarian,* vol.54, no.2, Summer 2006.

Lemaire, Kathy. *Shelf Life, Shelf Matters: Managing Resources in the School Library.* School Library Association, 2001. 978-1-903446-25-6.

Markless, Sharon (ed). *The Innovative School Librarian: Thinking Outside the Box.* Facet Publishing, 2009. 978-1-85604-653-4.

Museums Libraries and Archive Council. *Inspiring Learning For All.* MLA, 2008. Available at: http://www.inspiringlearningforall.gov.uk/

School Library Association. SLA Standards for Secondary School Libraries. 2011. Available at: http://www.sla.org.uk/

School Library Commission. *School Libraries: A Plan For Improvement.* School Library Commission chaired by Baroness Estelle Morris. 2010. Available at: http://www.literacytrust.org.uk/policy/nlt_policy/school_library_commission

Scottish Consultative Council on the Curriculum. *Taking a Closer Look at the School Library Resource Centre: Self-Evaluation Using Performance Indicators.* SCCC, 1999. 978-1-85955-848-5. Available at: http://www.svtc.org.uk/sccc/closer

Scottish Library and Information Council. *Improving Libraries for Learners? How good are we at supporting learning and meeting learning needs?* 2009. Available at: http://www.slainte.org.uk/files/pdf/slic/schoollibs/ImprovingLibsForLearners.pdf

Winkworth, Lynn and Dubber, Geoff. *Paperwork Made Easy: Policy Making and Development Planning for the Secondary School Library.* School Library Association, 2008. 978-1-903446-47-8.